Self-portrait

Also by Emanuel di Pasquale

Genesis (Boa Editions, 1989)
The Silver Lake Love Poems (Bordighera, 2000)
Escapes the Night (Gradiva Publications, 2001)
*Cartwheel to the Moon (*Cricket Books, 2003)
Europa (Gradiva Publications, 2006)
Writing Anew: New and Selected Poems (Bordighera, 2007)
Siciliana (Bordighera, 200(
Harvest (Bordighera 2011)
Out of Stars and Sand (Gradiva Publications, 2002)
*Love Lines (*Bordighera, 2013)
The Ocean's Will (Guernica, 2013)

Self-portrait

Poems by

Emanuel di Pasquale

The New York Quarterly Foundation, Inc.
New York, New York

NYQ Books™ is an imprint of The New York Quarterly Foundation, Inc.

The New York Quarterly Foundation, Inc.
P. O. Box 2015
Old Chelsea Station
New York, NY 10113

www.nyq.org

Copyright © 2014 by Emanuel di Pasquale

All rights reserved. No part of this book may be used or reproduced in any manner whatsoever without written permission of the author except in the case of brief quotations embodied in critical articles and reviews.

First Edition

Set in New Baskerville

Layout and Design by Joseph Hamersly
Cover Art by Franco Cilia | www.francocilia.com
          "Prima della notte," 2005, acrylic on canvas, 45 x 45 cm

Library of Congress Control Number: 2014934951

ISBN: 978-1-935520-88-7

Self-portrait

Acknowledgements

"Caught off the Metuchen, New Jersey, Train Station Wall" originally appeared in the *New York Quarterly*.

"Mad with Sweet John Clare" originally appeared in *The Sewanee Review*.

Contents

Self-Portrait /11
The Swim /12
Chiusura /13
Never Again Would Bird's Song Be the Same /14
Nightmare /15
A Gift /16
Open-Ended /17
Love is a Long Dawn /18
Love's Postscript /19
A Family /20
The Virgin's Curse /21
Fear and Hope /22
My Sea /23
Eden /24
Chimney Birds, for Michael Ganz /25
Windy First Day of Summer /26
A Message /27
M.C. Nurses a Baby Starling /28
Autumn Voyage /29
A Word of Advice /30
The Nature of Pain /31
A Certain Kind of Death /32
Death /33
Buried /34
The Hudson River /35
The Dead /36
God Is /37
Maya /38
Ancient Mountain Burials /39
Genesis /40

Caught Off the Metuchen, New Jersey, Train Station Wall   /41
Aurora, God's Wings   /42
A Student's Lament   /43
Early Fall, East Brunswick's Pond by the Public Library   /44
For My Father   /45
Death Comes   /46
Long Branch, Late August Windy—Wintry Day   /47
Kryseis   /48
The Dead Rise   /49
From the Mountain   /50
To a Woman, Agitated, As She Runs Out of a Mental Health Clinic   /53
The Sixth Sense   /54
Letter From Sicily   /55
Sunflower on Deep Run Road   /56
Cayuga Lake   /57
The Hurt Hawk   /58
Faith   /59
One for the Crow   /61
Mid-November in New Jersey   /62
Mid-March Night   /63
Reaching Out   /64
A Wonder   /65
Mad with Sweet John Clare   /66
Neighborly Care   /67
Night   /68
An Incantation   /69
The Lumberjack   /70
Morning Hawk   /71
Questions   /72

A Special Beast   / 73
For M. S.   / 74
Love Yet Fills The Bones   / 75
Spawning   / 76
To Edwin S. Godsey (poet, who in an attempt to save his son, died with the boy)   / 77
Ezra Pound, Ode   / 78
Sea/Winds   / 79
Venus   / 80
A Flurry of Love Poems   / 81
my prayer in age   / 83
My Buddha   / 84

Self-Portrait

What terror in your russet eyes,
Vincent. Mantled by brow
and hooded bone,
it leaps out of its socket
as if to distance itself from brain.

Is it all for the sin of color,
for seeing the northern lights in the swallow's flight,
for seeing a dry rain fall—
silvery, like guitar string bits?

Is it for seeing God both in the shut-in whore
and the peasant child as she
merges, like a violet iris, with her small garden?

Is it for seeing sheaves of wheat
lean like amber lovers?

Oh, Vincent, joy in the flux;
joy in the green blindness
that burns your brush blue.

Joy in the eye that fixes the vortex
of the yellow sun, in the spinning
of the diamond stars.

Joy in the cypress that swaggers
like a shaggy buffalo
in the angled prairie.

Joy in the church spire that rises into the sky;
Joy in the sky that flows its serpents into hills
 streams, firs

Joy in the almond blossoms,
 poppies

Joy in the dandelion brooks

The Swim

When the last boat has left
and all the bridges have fallen
from the rust of neglect or misuse
and you must cross
to the other side
of the miles-wide river
where the almond fields
and apple orchards flow
day by day
you will train for the long
inevitable swim

Weather won't matter
you'll train in rain
and storm
and glory in the challenge of hooked wave

One day
a bold move
and you'll crouch into the water and swim
straight and steadily for the other shore
giving in belly up to the current
as you reach the river's center

You will chance drowning
from tiredness cramps hungry eel
but you'll swim on
and if you'll have to drown
well then you'll drown
but there will be no turning back

Chiusura

A particular field of flowers—
poppies perhaps—red and tender-petaled in the wind
or a wheat field, children of the sun,
sperm spears
or a filament of sun
as it warmed me through
a kitchen window
or even the moonlight
as it sculptured an
empty pillow
or the smiling face of she
that once loved me both
for my gentleness and
fears.

Never Again Would Bird's Song Be the Same

The blue jay circled long and wide.
It stopped on tree, bush, browning grass
and chartered its eyes
to the empty nest
on the shining branch of a maple,
but could not trace its mate,
the lost she-bird.
It never used the nest again
but quickly built a new one
deep within a small thornbush.
All autumn long it stayed alone,
shooting out less and less song.
Then it left, coming back
at the first heavy snow,
eyeing the shining branch of maple,
singing loud song,
crash-landing
on pine trees,
shaking snow.

Nightmare

She said my body shook for a few seconds
before I woke up shouting, trembling. But
as our bedroom tumbled down brick by brick,
crumbled through asphalt street
into an underground river,
I lay frozen for hours,
fighting to scream out a word,
to trace a twitch on my face,
and let her know I lived.
And when I woke, the room still
half-shaking around me, I thought
of all the bodies that lay alive,
screaming within their minds,
settled into rootless graves
by disheveled lovers.

A Gift

You lick oleander leaves and
stick them on your fingers
"Eat, it's evergreen,"
your wet lips pray
How sweet the white flowers
How sweet the red flowers

Open-Ended

Give up all hope; then
wait for nothing.
Lost in that sea
say your prayers
and bless the seals
and gulls
and perhaps then
and only then
a ship will head
straight for you.

Love is a Long Dawn

My heart is the sea tonight—

Winds without end
Currents without end

Where do sea gulls huddle in this storm?
How deeply do fish dive?

Long is the night—
Longer still will be dawn…

Love's Postscript

It was no dream.
Dawn would wake up into each other's arms.
You'd moan and burrow your small body
in my belly and in my chest,
your head upon my heart,
your heat a soft sweet scent.
What has become of us?

A Family

When we close our eyes,
We are all turtles,
moles, dinosaurs,
Silurian snakes—
wrinkled in the grooves
of cosmic flow.

There is nothing to fear.
One step leads to another
just as one wave follows another
(at least as long as
moon follows earth
and earth follows sun).
We're in one pool,
one ocean.

The Virgin's Curse

While the moon loiters
in the late afternoon,
wearing a spotted,
see-through camisole,
the blinding sun flares
curlicues,
chartering red-tongued passageways,
but the moon,
pale girl,
wastes the night
lolling in the skies—
well out of the way
of the dragon-throated sun.

Fear and Hope

Like an eyelid closing,
a cloud slides under the sun
and turns morning
into early twilight.
Fear hoods me
like a monk's cape
pulled over a face,
over a head bent in mysteries!
But the winds
keep the cloud busy,
and the earth
holds on to its
yellows and gold.
Hope opens me
like a lava stream
stretching the floor
of the sea!

My Sea

Decembers ago,
having sailed through the Atlantic
and charted the throat of the Hudson,
my balls tucked by my belly button,
I ascended from the bowels
of the Vulcania
into Manhattan
while in my blood
sparkled
the salt of the Mediterranean.
(Oh, my sea,
clear as that lady's eyes.)
My sea,
wild white horses
where the cliffs between
Marina di Ragusa and Punta Secca
pushed into you—
stampeding manes in the
winds,
teeth tearing at the rocks,
throats neighing...

the gulls and a small boy
your witnesses.

Eden

Like a swallow,
the earth glides
on the ring of a blue horizon.
Great valleys cradle the seas,
and fishes freely swim
in our streams.
Horses gallop
on canyons and hills.
Our lovers' thighs
engulf us.
Children sleep in our arms.

Chimney Birds, for Michael Ganz

Ten birds in the year
will fly down the chimney
(the echo of beating wings,
cries of lost children
within that hollowness).

Something pulls them in—
the smell of fire in stone,
the such of wind.
Down through the throat they fall
and fly about the house.
None takes the open window out.
To let them go,
I catch them in my hands
and hold them like warm hearts.

Windy First Day of Summer

Today all the skies trees small roses
and low bushes are eagles and hawks.
The shadow of the tree branches
play seesaw on the ground.
Spent peonies lift their slim ears.
The few thin clouds, sea foam riding the skies,
sail quickly.

Moisture settles
into the silent roots and winds, large warm hands,
wipe off last night's rains from the necks
of cedars and oaks.

A Message

I will save this small feather,
so smooth, so simple.

It will recall the usefulness
of lost or thrown-out things.

M.C. Nurses a Baby Starling

After those few weeks of feeding the bird
water and bits of worms
and keeping its sense of flight
by waving its bare wings,
I had hoped it would come
back to the house
once it grew full-feathered
and was let go
to feed
and find joy in
its own source of flight.
It never did.
And if it had, a plain starling
among plain starlings
who could have picked it out?

Autumn Voyage

The leaves splash—
the wind the current,
the park the river bed,
my daughter and I
two kicking fish.

A Word of Advice

Among you there is
one who feels the heat of
stars in his veins,
one who knows the worm
as his brother, the starfish
as his sister; among you
there is one that prays
to the moving waters
of brooks, rivulets,
and rivers, one who whistles
the song of bluejay and cardinal, one
for whom the starling
returns year after
year; among you
there is one for whom babies smile and to
whom young children
run to, one
whose living eye
spooks the rabbi
and priest, one who
feasts at the joys of love.
Isolate him—quickly—
tear his guts open,
stone him,
drown him—
protect your dun limbs
from his glow.
Then go on your usual ways.

The Nature of Pain

God, was it you I saw
hunched on a branch,
a snow-clawed thing,
piping low
from under a broken wing?

A Certain Kind of Death

The horror of the tail cut off
From the warrior horse
From the pit bull
The horror of any Dragon
Submitting to Saint George
The horror of the Erect Snake
Crawling on its belly
Losing its supple limbs
Its wide wings

Death

Blue death shines like a halo over the dead dog;
It leaves him to sleep in too much peace,
And rushes into streams and the tops of trees.

Buried

We should be buried in forests,
In mountains, like leaves fallen into deep cracks,
The origins of brooks,
Rivers, rivulets

We should be buried far from the seas
And let the rains, our fathers,
Carry us in their fluid arms back home,
Into the mothers' spinning waves

The Hudson River

Thick ropes, the waters of the Hudson
Tie me, bind me, roll me from Albany
Down to New York City—
Like a free-falling log
Held in the current's tight hold.

The Dead

They wave at us
Old ladies leaning against companionable birches
Little girls in long white dresses
Men bent over like aged flowers
They wave at us
From a small island
In the middle of a lake so calm
Only the sun's reflecting gold gives the water life
Hands waving
                            Slowly
"We are here
Waiting
We are here"

God Is

for R. W. Emerson

Slate flakes into sand and dust

The robin sings

Waterfalls trill

Blue ocean currents curl red and white

Thighs open to thighs

A child looks open-eyed

Clouds weep to rain

Dirt and sunlight split open
The asparagus' head

Toes bend

Spine-bone churns blood cells

And Whitman gathers

Under my boot sole

Maya

The diviners make one mistake after another
They can't cure my restlessness
At least the earth gives you potatoes
If the rains come
If the sun radiates

I know the spirit is in the body, is the body
Perhaps a photograph can capture it
An X-ray for sure

Somewhere where balls and brain meet
In that liquidity that connects and heals

Oh, Pegasus, strike that rock hard,
Shatter it.

Ancient Mountain Burials

for John Keats

Masons cracked them open
For eternal reasons
In Ibla, Sicily,
Half way from the Rotunda
To the cemetery
And down into the riverless valley
Burial sheet
Bone
Blood
And flesh
Eaten by silence and time

Along the marble hills
Single burying cells
Small rectangles, squares
(empty eye sockets)
No bone survives
No ancient coin
No queenly necklace
No simple scratch to mark a name

Nothing survives
But empty eye sockets

Rock eggs

Genesis

The stars,
The unusual stars,
The stars that wanted to be, to see—
The large-eyed stars
That wanted to be seen

The emptiness that wanted to be filled,
That wanted to fill—
The stars
The dust that dreamed,
That spun itself into being—
The stars

Caught Off the Metuchen, New Jersey, Train Station Wall

I do not love you,
Isolyna Rivera
No more forever

Aurora, God's Wings

Does Black-Borealis come from light?
Does it have its own life?
Is death the back hand of life, or the palm?
Is sleep small death or life-driving, driven?
Eagles that mate in the high skies
And orgasm as they fall?
Does life blossom from the fall of death?
The burst of black that yearned to be seen, to see?

A Student's Lament

Five thousand years and thousands of gods,
Murder, incest, and nothing has changed.
We must accept mortality.
Be tight with our morality.
Be Enkidu or Patroclus
And die and pave the way
For haughty Gilgamesh or Achilles.
So much to read.
When all I want is wine
And hashish
Thousands of words
That I try to read
But stay mere words
I cannot even breathe
Let alone read
Thank god for pot
And wine

Early Fall, East Brunswick's Pond by the Public Library

for Steven Barnhart

The world of god metes out its sweet boredom
Not one tree is untouched by Fall
Bunches of leaves surrounded by brown halo
Small squirrels sniff and scratch soaked wood chips
The aerator shoots out
Three climbing waterfalls
So carp can keep on living
Geese work their wide wings
Croak and run across the pond
Signs for Peace, scarves,
Embrace a young birch
Next to a marble monument
For boys and girls lost to the last war

Inside the library
Sleek fans
Drones pinned to the ceiling
Scatter cool air

Measured click clock of heels
Of old woman ambling
To the latte counter
Fast flip flap of children
Rushing to computers
An aged man forming poetry
On two pink scraps of paper

For My Father

My father's coffin was no cedar—
It was the poor man's burying wood:
A few planks of uneven oak,
An old fig tree, and so his essence melted,
Mixing into the earth around his long rectangle—
And when his ten years of public burial
Came around, and he was dug out,
Skin still stuck to his bones,
Eyes to sockets, hair to skull—
Even his gray striped suit kept faith—
And his thin tongue still sang—
So said the grave keeper.

Death Comes

Death comes like a mother
Like a woman holding her child
By the fireplace
While the snow gathers heft
Tests the roof
As it packs into ice

Loose sparks find dry cracks,
Devour the house
And the flames embrace us,
Transmute us into cinders,
Into spires of fire,
And fly us home.

Long Branch, Late August Windy—Wintry Day

for X J Kennedy

When Frank Mullen's sons moved him
And his wife, Gerry, from their ocean home
To a park trailer in Freehold,
Frank looked at me, his mother-of-pearl
Eyeballs swimming in decades of beer and swill,
Lowered his head, and peeped, "Emanuel,
I will see you in heaven." And I sensed my own fate,
And saw it clearly today, in the pre-wintry chill
Of arrow northern rain—a couple blocks
From my ocean view: maroon paint torn
Annunciation—West End Manor—Motel Style
Bdrm—available. From its windowless rooms,
Non Si vedono le stelle. Otherwise, all is well.

Kryseis

Generous in all ways
Your sapphire eyes
Spin like the late afternoon's midway waves
On the eastern sea
As the early setting sun swirls
Rainbows into their spins—
Deep as longing
Deep as the pull of kiss
Or the joining of birds
And nest—
Open like an endless eddy your mind
The golden root of a black hole
That siphons into symphony—
Your tongue
Your hands make fire of my body

The Dead Rise

The dead rise recycled
galactic-eyed infants
Open wide
Rich in silences
Seeing watching
Waiting for the warm breasts of a mother
For the strong shoulders of a father
The dead come back
Bringing song
Bringing solar winds
Moon phases
The breath of ocean winds
Garbage heaps flowers
Dirt blossoms
The holiness of petals and filth

From the Mountain

I

Emily Dickinson walked deeply into it
Water like snakes swirling up her thighs, the sea
Sea gulls screech over it
Dive into it, rest on it
Fly over it standing still
Hold the wind under their wing, the sea—
Descend, descend, and find
The dunes, wheat fields churning bread
In the wind
The coo-coo birds singing the advent of
Spring

II

The divining rod
Will lead you to water
You can drink
(is dead Beatrice's hair
in the winds, or did
Dante fake the whole thing?)

III

See the dance
Of the rainbow's wanderings
When the sun spins west
And shoots over breaking waves
There there in the rainbow
Is the spirit
In the cracking spume

IV

Where is the reason in the snow?
Sugar and lemon
Make it ice cream—
A clean mix

The miracle of physics
And chemistry?
Water flowing at 33?

V

The gathering of wheat
At summer's end, presaging
The fall

Riding on a small donkey
To the farm
Stumping on wheat stalks
Scattering them to the sky
On late afternoons
Watching the chaff
Being eaten by the winds
The leftovers settling
On peach trees
Then the gathering of fallen grain
The trek to the wind mill
Flour and then bread

VI

Dark matter
Dark matter
Let me open your innards
Let's look into your womb
'a veder
La luce che sfolgora'
Just as there is
Light inside the hardest
Darkest seed
Just as there is light
Just as the cosmos is
Light and heat
Just as it congregates
Coagulates—
Each planet is a drop of blood
Each living sun
Energy churning
Attracting pulling
Small matter
Drawing it
into a solar tribe
Bivouacs
interspersed
And giving a center to the
universe.

To a Woman, Agitated, As She Runs Out of a Mental Health Clinic

You veer to your right,
into traffic,
holding your baby in your arms,
screaming at "bastards and
bitches." Your husband
tries to match your swift steps
and nudges you to your left,
where the car waits
like a tomb on wheels.
He orders you into
decorum. "Eleanor…
stop it…enough."
Your screams reach a higher
pitch. "How dare she?
The bitch…the bitch…"
You weep, and your baby,
close to your heart
and used to your confusion
and rage, does not wake.
My sister,
sufferer,
my sister.

The Sixth Sense

It is song:
the soft shiver of after love,
the sun within penis and vagina,
beak, swan, cloud,
river, rain.
It is the grain of sand,
the nebula,
needle of fir,
bleat of goat,
black hole,
touch,
flight of condor,
feather.

Letter From Sicily

We haven't stolen the grape
from the vineyard by the sea.
That creek where we used to wash
the stolen grape is dry;
the water loses itself
in the fields.

This summer even the hunt has grown stale.
Perhaps the rabbits have all hopped
to America to taunt hunters
braver than our hunters.

Return, dear friend,
for one more feast
on a hill,
under the stars,
where we may watch
our children dance.

Sunflower on Deep Run Road

Across a deserted gas pump,
fronting a children's
baseball field,
a sunflower
cocks its head
toward a farm
where birds sing
and where snakes slide
into rivulets.
I have spoken to it, and
in spinning waves
of yellow
and of blue,
it has spoken back.
It is. And in being, it licks stones into place,

Cayuga Lake

The lake knows something;
it knows no rush, nor does it know wait.
It tears rocks
cracks them into sand and smooths and swirls
them into pebbles.
It feels the weight of brown/red drakes
that chatter by shattered piers;
their bobbing is like the dry leaf rain of autumn.
It is without fear.
It is the water that leaps in thunderstorms,
the water that almost sleeps in late August.
It is. And in being, it opens to the naked body
of boy or girl—there, by the rushes—
it lets fishermen on white boats lighten its load.

City of silvery flash, of crab, turtle and fish,
the lake finds joy when the small child flies
into its waters,
as she holds her cat by her heart;
it opens for her,
swallows her feet first,
and, playing trampoline,
pushes her up head first.

The Hurt Hawk

Through the healing days,
the hurt hawk,
wing bent,
lives at the foot of the forest.
Restless, trapped
in the lessening of his
contained strength,
he lives in a makeshift
nest of weeds and leaves.
Each twilight
he struggles to the lake
and sips
the healing water.
By the waters he knows
he will fly
over the shine and ripple
of the depths
and dive
from joy.

Faith

Soldiers with limb like frost,
lost boys,
climb up from the shallow ditches,
swim up from the mile-long seas.

Father, Father,
Save us from
a Fall.

Father, Father,
Let Mother Bless
us all.

Soldiers with limbs like frost,
lost boys,
do not slouch, mechanical,
but pirouette to wild waltzes—
dance to the stars,
spin to the northern lights.

Father, Father,
Save us from
a Fall.

Father, Father,
Let Mother Bless
us all.

Soldiers with limbs like frost,
lost boys,
hose clean the slaughterhouse
of a Beelzebub named Hitler,
save the dreams of fields of poppies
charred by frost—
joy at the low skies,

bounce babies in your arms,
and catch them like falling birds.

Father, Father,
Save us from
a Fall.

Father, Father,
Let Mother Bless
us all.

One for the Crow

Morning peels the night out of the sky.
Stumbling like a pale sunray,
a crow flits, sits on a high, bent bough.
Wavering, like a living flame,
he caws. Fame, the leper with eyes
on the back of its skull,
passes him by,
as the horns and string of woods
and winds echo his song.

Mid-November in New Jersey

After a long silence,
a few birds sing.
They're back,
blue jay and
cardinal,
singing on
a darkening Monday
and I, on my
knees,
half-drowned in red
and yellow
leaves.

Mid-March Night

Last night, the north star danced
and shot swirling arms at me.
I walked out in the snow and
nodded and waved at my star—
my star that from far far away
danced and cavorted inside of me—
for something inside of me
did dance and swirl,
and my blood sang.

Reaching Out

There is a wonder that
over an ocean of deep breaths—
a swim,
a few hours sleep—
can soften muscles, brain,
the hold that like liquid nitrogen
freezes the body's blood.

There is a wonder
in the cleansing, freshening blood—
a creek's long tongue licking
cat and rabbit clean,
smoothing pebbles lean,
washing dull roots full.

A Wonder

In the season of sweet mulberry,
I was bending branches of the fruit,
when a woman, tresses long enough
to lasso high-flying birds,
settled on my shoulders.
Her hands crowded with the nearness of gods,
she fed me sweet mulberry.
And suddenly, I became xylem and phloem.
I became branches and fruit.

Mad with Sweet John Clare

Awake, John Clare, awake
and look for Mary Joyce.
Look for the angled sunray pounding light,
look for the lizard-tongued grass,
the hawk in open flight.

I want to be mad
and hold sweet John Clare by the hand
and all through Epping Forest learn to slither like the snakes
and grunt like the badgers
and learn with John
to bear to look at light
and live on hills
where the wild flower thrives
and look for Mary Joyce
in dewdrops and bluebells
and teach the dying child
to rip life clean,
to kill death with love.

Awake, John Clare, awake
and look for Mary Joyce.
Look for the angled sunray pounding light,
look for the lizard-tongued grass,
the hawk in open flight.

Neighborly Care

My neighbor, no doubt well-meaning,
has hung a BEWARE OF DOG sign on my side of the fence.
His dog, a hog free in a watermelon field,
barks at the sun and moon, my wife's old mother,
my children, straying bees, birds, and winds.

Amid the universe of Spring green,
my neighbor's sign pulls at my eyes.
Two years of sleeping half a stone's throw off,
and this is his only nod at my existence.
He has made the first move.
I answer by hanging a BEWARE OF CHILDREN sign
on his side of the fence.
The next move is his.
I load my .22.

Night

Sometime during the night,
there will be running
sounds in the empty attic,
and the young marrieds below
will start moving furniture.
Up on the hill,
the methodical trains
will hum by,
and the children will
have nightmares.
My wife or I
will double check
the door and balcony locks
and place
the great bouncing horse
before the door.

An Incantation

I could live among the small
white-headed gulls
and the fish stuck in the mud
in the low tide

I could live
praising stones
and the moon rise

I could live
burning small fish
black
over a few sticks

I could live

The Lumberjack

That humans aren't trees,
though they fall like spear-split eyes,
drilled teeth and jaw
of the first dead of the first skirmish,
last laid corpse of the last war,
is not seen by the lumberjack,
he of the fat bicep.
That skulls don't blossom
and that the death of babes
is no bud, winds burn
and no Spring revives,
is not seen by the lumberjack,
he of the fat bicep.

Morning Hawk

The hawk flew over my house
and veered to his right.
The feathers, the small feathers
on the wing tips—
did they wave at me?

Questions

Why do we bury our children
in baskets made of hay?

Why do our old women crawl
on bleeding knees
to marble altars?

What makes the forest sing,
the Amazon whisper its damp moan?

Why can't we reap grain
for our bread?

Why are our cool amphorae
cracked and our rivers dry?
How shall we drink?

Why do lovers after the first heat
turn to silence and cold clay?

A Special Beast

When Mary Magdalene first saw Christ fix the dirty crowd
with his eyes, his fingers reaching out for her,
shutting her fears,
she saw in him the fire of the unicorn.

A few nights later,
when she could finally snatch him
away for an hour or two
from women that pecked at him
as tribes of starlings peck at grain,
she mentioned the fire she had seen.

And he, always holding her
in his eyes, said,
"I am both the unicorn and the snake."

For M. S.

I.

The seagulls huddle on the gray shore, still,
and throughout morning angle their bodies to the sun.
By noon, the skies brimming with crabs and fish
that flash silver, the gulls fly, their wings beating a sacrament—
their throats free in the joy of song—
children measuring the breaking wave.

Lost in the winter dawn of a gray sea,
I angle my thoughts to your flight, your song—
your eyes like the streaks of highest ocean,
your voice the trill of a she-dolphin.
Where are you, Madelyn? Be sea,
bluefish, she-dolphin, seagull, sun.

II.

The November moon, its upper half torn,
leans into the ocean and fills it with silver lizards
that swim northwest and keep the waters lapping.

Follow their train, Madelyn, and once more
find your way to Long Branch, blue and jutting out—
too cold, too still because it misses your body
with its rippling walk of fawn.

Love Yet Fills The Bones

Tear innards
and feed them
to the fires

Take heart
and hurl it
at starlings and blackbirds

Saw skull
and let brain turn
to leather in the sun

Love yet fills the bones,
suffuses flesh

Spawning

The cutthroat trout
large-eyed
circles downstream
in the drowned eddies
till it turns and rising leaps
into the tongue-white-silver falls and leaps and leaps
falls over
falls over
falls

To Edwin S. Godsey (poet, who in an attempt to save his son, died with the boy)

You move on the swing
of energy swirls,
you and your son—
helping each other climb
little hills,
howling at slips,
offering hands at the crossings
of small rivers.
On the swing of energy swirls,
you and your son move
where myriad children
continually wander.

Ezra Pound, Ode

Night heftily nearing,
clucking offers of stillness
and you fully silent,
you, who yet have your mind entire
(a map of Manhattan on the inner
fold of your gypsy hat,
mixing pages of Keats and Whitman),
listen to newspapermen, columnists,
Actaeon-eyed, and from you emerges
an assenting nod or nothing.
An idling machine in front
of a red semaphore,
you stand, entire.
Your beauty shall be unbroken.
Your dust with Waller's and
more than Waller's shall be laid.

Sea/Winds

How like the sounds of open seas—
the winds on all these trees.

Venus

From far away,
a blue-eyed child,
emerald mild.

From up up close,
no children sing by waterwells,
no raindrops swell.

A Flurry of Love Poems

I.

As the better poet sings,
that walk of hers
circles upon circles
it churns wheat
it sings

II.

The small noises your throat makes
a seagull's wing bent over the wide shore
the wind as ornament
over a mum's spare-leaved stem

III.

Your hips that simply by moving speak
(How one black bird can squander your sweet sound)
Hear how our children chirp
(Are we all birds at birth?)

IV.

To die, rock heavy,
in the full rain
next to a pregnant river
on the left bank—
light as the breaking
moonlight

V.

Just as I miss you
must death miss life
My darkness is all light
when I see you

VI.

Ah, but you must have your way
or else
long silences or moans
tightening of your heart
all all is gloom
The busy moon spins out of sight
the sun rushes into night

VII.

"You are no Shakespeare," you say.
"There is no Tempest in your sea."
True, but like his
my lyrical breath
will kill death

my prayer in age

my strength fails
who shall care for me
my children have their own children who need caring
and my younger child is like a sapling,
a young birch,
who herself needs tending
who shall right my limbs
as they falter and bend with pain
and who shall care for my eyes
that burn and hurt
who shall right my hand
as it trembles
my heart as it beats
too fast

My Buddha

I will let my silence
be my screams
my peace my terror
my dry eye my tears
I will let the ocean
be my desert
the full moon my darkness
and your open face
my blindness
and all that lives and breathes:
lady bug cat dandelion
weed sea gull
brown eyes
prickly sting of rose
be my paradise

The New York Quarterly Foundation, Inc.
New York, New York

Poetry Magazine
Since 1969

Edgy, fresh, groundbreaking, eclectic—voices from all walks of life.

Definitely NOT your mama's poetry magazine!

The *New York Quarterly* has been defining the term contemporary American poetry since its first craft interview with W. H. Auden.

Interviews • Essays • and of course, lots of poems.

www.nyq.org

No contest! That's correct, NYQ Books are NO CONTEST to other small presses because we do not support ourselves through contests. Our books are carefully selected by invitation only, so you know that NYQ Books are produced with the same editorial integrity as the magazine that has brought you the most eclectic contemporary American poetry since 1969.

Books

www.nyq.org

poetry at the edge™

Emanuel di Pasquale was born in Ragusa, Sicily, and emigrated to America in 1957. His translations from Italian include *The Journey Ends Here* by Carlo della Corte (Gradiva, 2000), *Sharing a Trip* by Silvio Ramat (Bordighera Press, 2001), which won a Raiziss/dePalchi Fellowship from the Academy of American Poets, and *Between the Blast Furnaces and the Dizziness* by Milo De Angelis (Chelsea Editions, 2003). He has published sixteen books of his own poetry, the first being *Genesis* (Boa Editions, 1989); and the latest four being *Siciliana* (2009), *Harvest* (2011), *Love Lines* (2013) from Bordighera Press, and *The Ocean's Will* (2013) from Guernica Editions (Canada). He has also written a book for children, *Cartwheel to the Moon* (Cricket Books, 2003). In 2012 Xenos books published his translation of Dante's *La Vita Nova* which he co-translated with Bruno Alemanni, and Gradiva Publications published his poetry book *Out of Stars and Sand and other Sicilian Poems*.

CPSIA information can be obtained
at www.ICGtesting.com
Printed in the USA
BVOW04s0312200517
484450BV00004B/41/P